Civil War Forts

Untold History of the Civil War

CHELSEA HOUSE PUBLISHERS

Untold History of the Civil War

Civil War Forts

Victor Brooks

CHELSEA HOUSE PUBLISHERS
Philadelphia

Produced by Combined Publishing
P.O. Box 307, Conshohocken, Pennsylvania 19428
1-800-418-6065
E-mail:combined@combinedpublishing.com
web:www.combinedpublishing.com

CHELSEA HOUSE PUBLISHERS

Editor in Chief: Stephen Reginald
Managing Editor: James D. Gallagher
Production Manager: Pamela Loos
Art Director: Sara Davis
Director of Photography: Judy L. Hasday
Senior Production Editor: LeeAnne Gelletly
Assistant Editor: Anne Hill

Front Cover Illustration: Courtesy of the National Park Service,
    artist, L. Kenneth Townsend

The Chelsea House World Wide Web site address is
http://www.chelseahouse.com

First Printing

1 3 5 7 9 8 6 4 2

Library of Congress Cataloging-in-Publication Data applied for:
ISBN 0-7910-5438-1

Contents

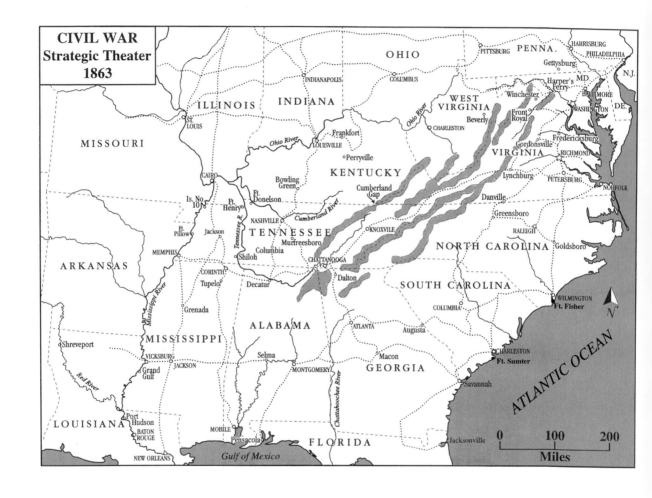

CIVIL WAR
Strategic Theater
1863

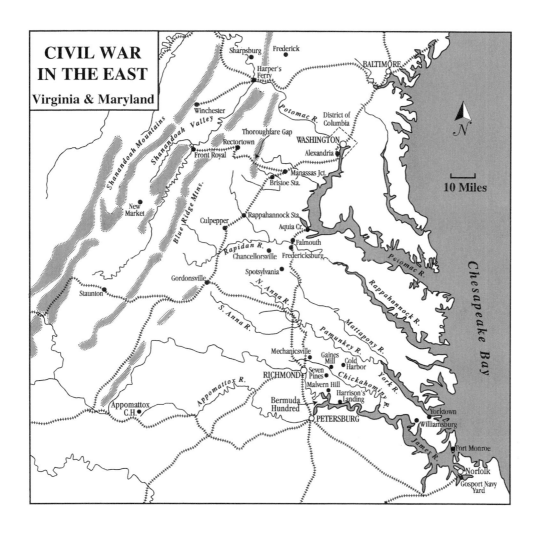

CIVIL WAR IN THE EAST

Virginia & Maryland

Sharpsburg
Frederick
BALTIMORE
Harper's Ferry
Winchester
Potomac R.
District of Columbia
WASHINGTON
Thoroughfare Gap
Rectortown
Alexandria
Front Royal
Manassas Jct.
Bristoe Sta.
Shanandoah Mountains
Shanandoah Valley
Blue Ridge Mtns.
New Market
Rappahannock Sta.
10 Miles
Culpepper
Rappahannock Sta.
Aquia Cr.
Rapidan R.
Falmouth
Chancellorsville
Fredericksburg
Staunton
Gordonsville
Spotsylvania
Potomac R.
Rappahannock R.
N. Anna R.
S. Anna R.
Mattapony R.
Pamunkey R.
Mechanicsville
Gaines Mill
Cold Harbor
Chesapeake Bay
RICHMOND
Seven Pines
Chickahominy R.
York R.
Malvern Hill
Harrison's Landing
Appomattox R.
Appomattox C.H.
Bermuda Hundred
Yorktown
Williamsburg
PETERSBURG
James R.
Fort Monroe
Norfolk
Gosport Navy Yard

N

Civil War Chronology

1860

November 6   Abraham Lincoln is elected president of the United States.

December 20   South Carolina becomes the first state to secede from the Union.

1861

January-April   Mississippi, Florida, Alabama, Georgia, Louisiana, and Texas also secede from the Union.

April 1   Bombardment of Fort Sumter begins the Civil War.

April-May   Lincoln calls for volunteers to fight the Southern rebellion, causing a second wave of secession with Virginia, Arkansas, Tennessee, and North Carolina all leaving the Union.

May   Union naval forces begin blockading the Confederate coast and reoccupying some Southern ports and offshore islands.

July 21   Union forces are defeated at the battle of First Bull Run and withdraw to Washington.

1862

February   Previously unknown Union general Ulysses S. Grant captures Confederate garrisons in Tennessee at Fort Henry (February 6) and Fort Donelson (February 16).

March 7-8   Confederates and their Cherokee allies are defeated at Pea Ridge, Arkansas.

March 8-9   Naval battle at Hampton Roads, Virginia, involving the USS *Monitor* and the CSS *Virginia* (formerly the USS *Merrimac*) begins the era of the armored fighting ship.

April-July   The Union army marches on Richmond after an amphibious landing. Confederate forces block Northern advance in a series of battles. Robert E. Lee is placed in command of the main Confederate army in Virginia.

April 6-7   Grant defeats the Southern army at Shiloh Church, Tennessee, after a costly two-day battle.

April 27   New Orleans is captured by Union naval forces under Admiral David Farragut.

May 31   The battle of Seven Pines (also called Fair Oaks) is fought and the Union lines are held.

August 29-30   Lee wins substantial victory over the Army of the Potomac at the battle of Second Bull Run near Manassas, Virginia.

September 17   Union General George B. McClellan repulses Lee's first invasion of the North at Antietam Creek near Sharpsburg, Maryland, in the bloodiest single day of the war.

November 13   Grant begins operations against the key Confederate fortress at Vicksburg, Mississippi.

December 13   Union forces suffer heavy losses storming Confederate positions at Fredericksburg, Virginia.

1863

January 1   President Lincoln issues the Emancipation Proclamation, freeing the slaves in the Southern states.

May 1-6	Lee wins an impressive victory at Chancellorsville, but key Southern commander Thomas J. "Stonewall" Jackson dies of wounds, an irreplaceable loss for the Army of Northern Virginia.
June	The city of Vicksburg and the town of Port Hudson are held under siege by the Union army. They surrender on July 4.
July 1-3	Lee's second invasion of the North is decisively defeated at Gettysburg, Pennsylvania.
July 16	Union forces led by the black 54th Massachusetts Infantry attempt to regain control of Fort Sumter by attacking the Fort Wagner outpost.
September 19-20	Confederate victory at Chickamauga, Georgia, gives some hope to the South after disasters at Gettysburg and Vicksburg.

1864

February 17	A new Confederate submarine, the *Hunley*, attacks and sinks the USS *Housatonic* in the waters off Charleston.
March 9	General Grant is made supreme Union commander. He decides to campaign in the East with the Army of the Potomac while General William T. Sherman carries out a destructive march across the South from the Mississippi to the Atlantic coast.
May-June	In a series of costly battles (Wilderness, Spotsylvania, and Cold Harbor), Grant gradually encircles Lee's troops in the town of Petersburg, Richmond's railway link to the rest of the South.
June 19	The siege of Petersburg begins, lasting for nearly a year until the end of the war.
August 27	General Sherman captures Atlanta and begins the "March to the Sea," a campaign of destruction across Georgia and South Carolina.
November 8	Abraham Lincoln wins reelection, ending hope of the South getting a negotiated settlement.
November 30	Confederate forces are defeated at Franklin, Tennessee, losing five generals. Nashville is soon captured (December 15-16).

1865

April 2	Major Petersburg fortifications fall to the Union, making further resistance by Richmond impossible.
April 3-8	Lee withdraws his army from Richmond and attempts to reach Confederate forces still holding out in North Carolina. Union armies under Grant and Sheridan gradually encircle him.
April 9	Lee surrenders to Grant at Appomattox, Virginia, effectively ending the war.
April 14	Abraham Lincoln is assassinated by John Wilkes Booth, a Southern sympathizer.

Union Army
Army of the Potomac
Army of the James
Army of the Cumberland

Confederate Army
Army of Northern Virginia
Army of Tennessee

I

Fort Sumter:
The Ring of Fire

When a person mentions Civil War battles, many people imagine thousands of men in blue and gray charging fiercely up rocky ridges or firing at one another through tree-covered fields. Yet some of the most dramatic confrontations of the Civil War occurred when the two armies were fighting for possession of a brick, or stone, or even sand stronghold that had been built as a fort by either Yankees or Rebels. By 1861 there were already famous forts in American history from Fort Ticonderoga to Fort McHenry to the Alamo. However, during the next four years there would be dozens of battles and sieges in which Union and Confederate troops struggled to gain control of walled strongpoints that ranged in size from imposing fortresses to hastily constructed barricades. Five forts played a major role in some of the most dramatic moments of the Civil War. From Fort Sumter on the Atlantic Ocean to Vicksburg on the Mississippi River, each of these contests was a key point in the titanic struggle that we call the Civil War.

Below is one of the large cannons of Fort Moultrie. The fort was deemed indefensible and abandoned by the few Union soldiers left to guard it.

On the day after Christmas of 1860, Captain Abner Doubleday of the United States Army climbed the steps to the parapets of Fort Moultrie, South Carolina, and peered across the harbor to watch the bustling activity in the nearby city of Charleston. Twenty years earlier, Abner Doubleday had gained recognition when he had helped to formalize the rules of the new game of baseball in Cooperstown, New York, but now the young artillery officer faced a much more serious challenge. He was second in command of the Federal garrison in a harbor that now technically belonged to

a foreign country. Six days earlier, a convention of South Carolina delegates had voted that the union between their state and the United States of America was "forever dissolved" and that they now lived in an independent republic. Now, many people in Charleston were calling for the use of force to evict the 82 blue-coated soldiers who each morning continued to raise the Stars and Stripes over Fort Moultrie's walls. Captain Doubleday knew that the secessionists could call on almost 7,000 South Carolina militiamen if force was used, and in that case, the Federal troops would be lucky to last an hour.

The man responsible for raising the American flag over Charleston Harbor each day was the commanding officer of Fort Moultrie, Major Robert Anderson. Anderson's father had helped defend Fort Moultrie against the British during the American Revolution but now his son was caught in two terrible dilemmas. First, Major Anderson was a Southern man who had married into a family of important Georgia slaveholders. Anderson strongly opposed Abraham Lincoln's election and believed that the South was right in the current crisis over slavery. On the other hand, he had sworn an oath to protect the constitution of the United States and he still felt obligated to that oath. Major Anderson's second challenge was even more immediate. He was commanding a fort that was almost indefensible. Fort Moultrie had been built next to a seashore town in which enemy snipers could easily climb to the second floor windows of local houses and actually fire down onto the men defending the fort. Also, sand had been allowed to drift up against the walls of the fort for so long that in many places cattle would simply walk over the dunes into the fort when they were looking for good grazing spots. Robert Anderson probably commanded the most undefendable fort in America and yet the first battle of a coming war would be fought in this harbor.

A few minutes after Abner Doubleday surveyed the scene in Charleston Harbor from the ramparts of Fort Moultrie, he knocked on Major Anderson's office door to invite the fort's commander to an afternoon tea hosted by Doubleday's wife. However, when he was ushered into the office, the artillery captain was given shocking news by his superior. Within 20 minutes the garrison of Fort Moultrie would begin evacuating the fort and be rowed across a mile of open water to an unfinished fort that loomed in the middle of Charleston Harbor—Fort Sumter. Major Anderson had no intention of allowing the secessionists to overwhelm his men in this undefendable structure; the

Fort Sumter in Charleston Harbor was the site of the first battle of the Civil War.

bluecoats would make their stand in a fort where they might at least have some chance.

As the sun began to set on this short winter afternoon, two companies of blue-coated troops marched quietly through the streets of the adjoining town of Moultrieville and then clambered into three rowboats waiting to push off from a small cove. Doubleday's boat was nearly to Fort Sumter when a South Carolina patrol boat suddenly appeared uncomfortably close by. Armed lookouts peered from the deck of the patrol boat through the gathering darkness and the Federal artillery captain quickly took off his military hat and unbuttoned his coat to hide the brass buttons. He whispered to his men to hide their muskets and remove their caps. After a few minutes of tension, the lookouts assumed that the small boat was merely taking some of Sumter's workmen back to Charleston and the rowboat started again as the patrol boat moved off into the night. A few minutes later, after breathing sighs of relief at their narrow escape, the blue-coated soldiers from Fort Moultrie entered the fort that would be their home for the next several months.

Fort Sumter was both old and new at the same time. The huge five-sided fortress had actually been started in 1829, but now over 30 years later it was still not quite finished. The fort had been built on an artificial island with New Hampshire and Maine granite and

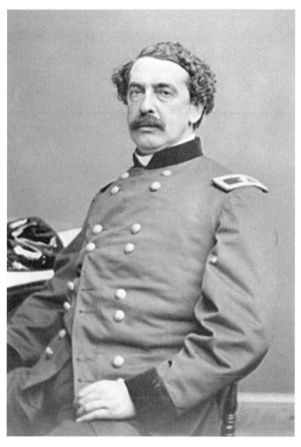

Abner Doubleday fired the first Union shot of the Civil War at Fort Sumter on April 13, 1861.

Major Robert Anderson was the commander of Fort Sumter at the start of the Civil War.

featured walls that towered nearly 50 feet above its acre-sized parade ground. Fort Sumter was designed to hold 135 cannons in three levels of gun ports: two tiers of arched rooms called casemates and an upper parapet level on the top of the walls. The fort was designed to hold a garrison of 650 men who were expected to coordinate their activities with other forts around the harbor if Charleston was ever threatened by an enemy war fleet. However, as Anderson and his men entered Sumter on this chilly December evening, only 15 cannons had actually been put in place by workmen while 45 other guns were strewn at crazy angles throughout the fort. Given time, all of these other weapons could eventually be mounted, but in order to defend this huge fortress Major Anderson had exactly 61 artillerymen, 13 members of a regimental band, 7 officers, and 1 junior surgeon under his command.

While Major Anderson and Captain Doubleday expected that the secessionists would attack Fort Sumter as soon as they discovered Fort Moultrie had been abandoned, cooler heads prevailed and no shots were fired. However, over the next several weeks, South Carolina joined with six other states that had seceded to form the Confederate States of America and the new Confederate president, Jefferson Davis, sent one of his new generals to besiege Fort Sumter. Pierre Beauregard was a Louisiana graduate of West

Point who had enrolled in Major Anderson's course at school and then had joined the faculty at the major's recommendation. Now he was building what he called a "ring of fire" around his old teacher and friend. When Abraham Lincoln was inaugurated as the 16th president of the United States in March of 1861, the Fort Sumter issue became his main crisis. Jefferson Davis emphasized that it was intolerable for his new nation to accept a foreign flag waving in the middle of one of the Confederacy's biggest harbors and if that flag was not soon removed, Beauregard's cannons would force Anderson to leave.

At 3:30 P.M. on the morning of April 12, 1861, three of General Beauregard's aides rowed out to Fort Sumter and informed Major Anderson that unless he agreed to evacuate the fort, Confederate batteries would

The interior of Fort Sumter. To the right you can see the arched rooms called casemates.

begin to fire in one hour. Anderson escorted the aides back to Fort Sumter's small dock, and in a choked voice whispered, "If we never meet in this world again, God grant that we may meet in the next." Sixty minutes later a shell arched slowly in the humid, predawn darkness and glowed a dull red as it descended over Fort Sumter. Hundreds of Charleston's citizens had climbed to their rooftops or gathered along the city's promenade to watch history in the making, and as the first shot exploded over the Federal fort, people displayed a huge range of emotions from joy to tears. The bloodiest war in American history was now underway.

Fort Sumter was bombed by an overwhelming force of Confederates until the Union soldiers surrendered.

For the next three hours over 50 Southern cannons sent shells screaming into Fort Sumter while Major Anderson ordered his men to hold their fire until it was light enough to see Confederate targets. Finally, at 7:30 A.M. Captain Abner Doubleday personally aimed one of Sumter's cannons and fired the first Union shot of the Civil War. For the rest of this cloudy, sultry Friday morning and afternoon, a tiny force of six Federal cannons fought a very unequal duel with almost 10 times as many Rebel guns. Most of the fort's more powerful weapons were mounted on the open parapets, but, in order to prevent casualties, Anderson limited his fire to the better protected, but smaller, casemate guns. Since Beauregard had ordered most of the Confederate batteries reinforced with either dozens of cotton bales or thick strips of railroad iron, Union gunners were frustrated trying to hit the enemy. One Federal officer insisted that Sumter's cannons had about the same effect on enemy batteries as a peashooter fired at a brick wall. The fight was so one-sided that by Friday afternoon even the Confederate soldiers were often cheering the Federal gunners just for the fact that they were still in the fight.

By Friday evening, while Fort Sumter was still in Federal hands, it was becoming clear to people on both sides that the fort couldn't last much longer. Sumter had a large number of wooden building and now each of them was on fire as flames sparked in the night sky. On Saturday morning, April 13, the Stars and Stripes was still defiantly waving over the fort, but gunners were gasping for breath as smoke filled the casemates and a major fire was running out of control and creeping toward Sumter's main powder magazine. General Beauregard was now genuinely concerned about the safety of his old teacher and his men, and he sent several of his aides to the fort to ask Major Anderson if he needed any help in fighting the spreading flames. His messengers also carried a very generous surrender proposal, and when Anderson looked around at his burning fort, he decided to accept Beauregard's terms.

The next day, Sunday, April 14, 1861, as Charleston boat operators took citizens on tours around Sumter's walls at 50 cents a person, Major Robert Anderson ordered a final 100-gun salute to the American flag before it was taken down. Halfway through the impressive ceremony, a flying spark dropped into a supply of gunpowder and a ferocious explosion rocked the parade ground. Moments later, Private Daniel Hough died of injuries from the explosion, becoming the first American to die in the Civil War. Miraculously, in the two day battle for Fort Sumter, no one from either army had been killed or even seriously injured. Now, as a Confederate chaplain offered prayers and a South Carolina honor guard saluted, the first man killed in what would be a bloody war was buried. As his men prepared to march out of Fort Sumter for a waiting transport steamer, Major Anderson hauled down the American flag and reverently placed the national emblem in his pocket.

Exactly four years to the day later, on Good Friday, April 14, 1865, General Robert Anderson would salute a group of dignitaries who had gathered in newly recaptured Fort Sumter and raised the same flag over the fort. The man who was perhaps the most responsible for this joyous occasion, Abraham Lincoln, was invited to sail down from Washington for this symbolic gesture. However, the president reluctantly declined the invitation and instead met another destiny as he sat in Ford's Theater on that awful Friday evening.

II

Forts Henry and Donelson:
Siege in the Snow

*T*he firing on Fort Sumter plunged Americans into a war in which many relatives and old friends found themselves on opposite sides in the struggle between Union and Confederacy. One friendship affected by the war was between Simon Bolivar Buckner and Ulysses S. Grant. Buckner and Grant had been comrades in the war with Mexico. Several years later when Grant's drinking problems had wrecked his army career and emptied his bank account, Buckner had loaned the disgraced officer the money to pay his passage home, a favor that the rumpled midwesterner would never forget. However, by the beginning of 1862, Buckner was fighting to ensure that his beloved state of Kentucky would become part of the Confederacy while Grant had just been placed in command of an army whose mission was to keep the bluegrass state and its southern neighbor of Tennessee members of the Federal union.

Both Union and Confederate generals had spent the first months of the Civil War raising and training

The Confederate army surrendered Fort Donelson on February 16, 1862.

armies, but by early in 1862 Federal armies in the west were about ready to move southward. One of the first targets for a Northern offensive was the important Tennessee capital city of Nashville. Nashville boasted one of the largest war factories in the Confederacy and served as a major communications and railroad center for much of the South. The new commander of

Confederate troops in the western department, General Albert Sydney Johnston, was very aware of what the Federals were planning, and he knew that the key to the campaign would be control of the Tennessee and Cumberland Rivers; these twin streams that paralleled each other much of their length, were the gateways to Tennessee from the state of Kentucky to the north. Any Federal army that was expecting to lunge toward Nashville from the north would have to control access to these rivers. In order to keep these vital waterways in Rebel hands, General Johnston had ordered his engineers to build two major forts near the Tennessee-Kentucky border; Fort Henry guarded access to the Tennessee River, while Fort Donelson stood sentinel over the Cumberland River, 12 miles to the east.

Ulysses Grant knew that the Rebels were building forts to block a drive south from Kentucky, but the Union general and his navy counterpart, Commodore Andrew Foote, were convinced that a combined land-water attack using bluecoat troops and naval gunboats could capture both forts and open the way to Nashville. On January 30, 1862, Grant's superior, General Henry Halleck, telegraphed permission to begin marching south and despite a raging blizzard howling outside their headquarters, Grant and Foote and their staffs threw hats into the air and pounded each other on the back. The first major western offensive of the Civil War was about to begin!

As 23 regiments of infantry and a small fleet of gunboats pushed south through sleet and snow, the defenders of Fort Henry waited grimly for the expected confrontation. On paper, the fort guarding the Tennessee River looked formidable. General Lloyd Tilghman had crammed over 3,000 soldiers and dozens of cannons into Fort Henry and the troops

General Lloyd Tilghman, the Confederate leader at Fort Henry, decided to evacuate most of his men before the Union assault began.

were protected by thick, high walls. However, as winter brought fierce snowstorms and torrential downpours almost one after another, General Tilghman began to realize that the Confederate engineers had made a terrible mistake. The Rebel fort was first constructed during one of the driest periods of the year, but by early February of 1862 the constant storms had pushed the now raging Tennessee River to its highest flood point in 50 years. Whole sections of the fort were underwater, most of the gun emplacements had been flooded, and messengers entered the main gate of the fort in rowboats instead of horses. Even worse, spies were reporting to the Confederate general that Foote's gunboats were not vulnerable wooden boats but revolutionary new ironclads that would be extremely hard to sink.

Tilghman decided on a desperate plan. Almost all of his infantry regiments would be evacuated the 12 miles to Fort Donelson to heavily reinforce the graycoats who were already stationed there. However, enough Rebel gunners would remain behind to operate the nine remaining cannons that were not yet covered with water. General Tilghman would remain behind with the small force and either die or surrender with the men he called a "forlorn hope."

On the morning of February 9, 1862, one of the first sunny days in weeks, Commodore Foote's "turtleback" gunboats steamed slowly toward the Confederate fort as captains squinted to see what might

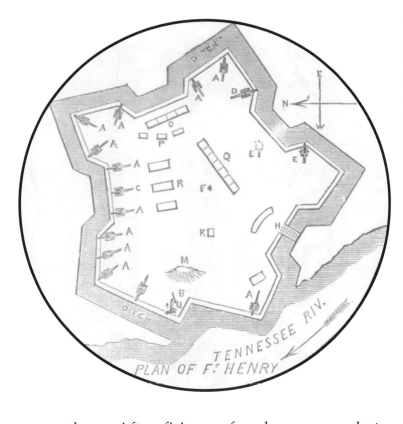

PLAN OF F: HENRY

This plan of Fort Henry appeared in Harper's Weekly *in 1862. It shows the fort's location on the Tennessee River that caused it to flood and the positioning of its artillery.*

oppose them. After firing a few long-range shots, Foote's flotilla moved to within 600 yards of the flooded fort and let loose with 52 guns that one defender described as "one broad and leaping sheet of flame." Even at this fairly short distance, most of the Rebel guns, were too small to have much impact on the Yankee ships' armorplating, but two cannons were able to make their presence felt. A giant "Columbiad" that could fire a huge, 128-pound shell and a high velocity, 6-inch rifled cannon pounded the gunboats with a number of serious hits. The ironclad *Essex* took a shot through her boiler that left eight men screaming from scalding, escaping steam and the ship veered out of control. However, just as the two guns started to make serious trouble, both of them suffered malfunctions that knocked them out of the battle. One by one,

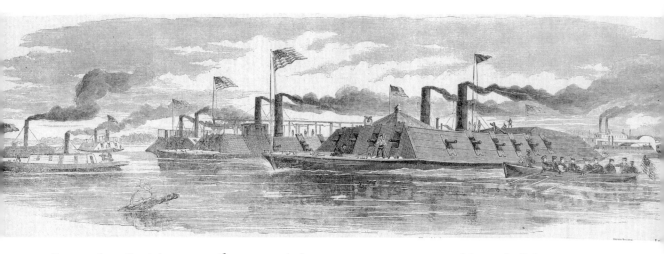

Commodore Foote's flotilla of ironclads steams toward Fort Donelson.

the remaining seven guns capable of firing were knocked out by the gunboats and General Tilghman decided it was now time to surrender. A United States navy launch poked its way through the main gate of the fort and a naval officer was rowed to Tilghman's headquarters to receive the surrender. One of the two main obstacles to a Yankee capture of Nashville was now flying the United States flag.

Ulysses Grant was happy with the surrender of Fort Henry but disappointed that the navy and not the army had accepted the Rebel surrender. Now the Union army would get its chance for glory in the march to Fort Donelson. For a brief time, the frigid, wet weather receded, and soon blue-coated soldiers were marching toward the Cumberland River in almost summer-like warmth. Thousands of blankets and overcoats littered the main road between the two rivers as Yankee troops assumed that the winter was over. However, reality began to set in as the Federals approached Fort Donelson. First, the Confederate high command had rushed thousands of reinforcements to the fort's nearby port of Dover, and soon the expeditionary force of 15,000 bluecoats was being faced by a Rebel army of close to 20,000 men. Then, the spring-like weather abruptly ended and by the evening of February 13 snow was falling furiously and the temperature was plunging toward 10 degrees.

By Valentine's Day morning, thousands of half-frozen bluecoats were longing for their abandoned blankets and overcoats as they watched Commodore Foote's gunboat squadron steam down the Cumberland to try for a repeat of the Fort Henry victory. This time the Yankee fleet was facing a fort that was not half underwater, and much of the flotilla was undergoing repairs from a terrible pounding. At this low point for the Union offensive, the three Confederates responsible for defending Fort Donelson arrived at a fateful decision. A strange complication of orders from the Confederate government left Generals John Floyd, Gideon Pillow, and Simon Bolivar Buckner in some confusion about who was actually responsible for guarding the Cumberland fort. However, the three men soon agreed that Grant had about 40,000 men outside Fort Donelson, twice as many as they commanded. They didn't know that Union reinforcements were actually pouring into Fort Henry very rapidly, but most of these units hadn't begun to march over the icy road that connected the rivers and there were actually more Rebels than Yankees around Fort Donelson itself. The three Confederate generals decid-

Commodore Andrew Foote led the Union's naval bombardments of forts Henry and Donelson.

ed to launch a huge surprise attack on the Federals at dawn on Saturday morning. They hoped that their men could punch a hole in the Federal lines and allow the graycoats to escape and march across country toward safety at Nashville.

February 15, 1862, dawned frigid and blustery as thousands of Rebel troops advanced through the eerie quiet of the snowcovered ground toward the nearby Federal lines. A few of the Rebel units had even been equipped for fighting in the snow; one Kentucky regiment had been outfitted in light-colored, hooded parkas and heavily lined boots that Russian soldiers would have welcomed. As blue-coated soldiers stood half-frozen around their campfires, shots started to pierce the frigid air and suddenly, swarms of Rebels were overrunning exposed Yankee units. General Grant was back at Fort Henry conferring with Commodore Foote when messengers came galloping toward the naval flagship to tell the Union leaders the frightening news. While Grant mounted a horse and hurried eastward as fast as the glazed roads would allow, one of his subordinates began directing the Federal defense of their siege lines.

General Lew Wallace would become famous as a writer 20 years later when he wrote the enormously popular novel *Ben-Hur.* Now, however, on this freezing February morning, the future best-selling author cooly issued orders and rushed blue-coated units to points where the Confederates threatened to break through. By the time Grant arrived on the scene, the tide was just beginning to turn, and soon the army commander was directing a counterattack that threw the Rebels back into their defense lines. For one brief period the road to Nashville had been open, but the Confederate generals had been too slow to react and now their opponent held the upper hand.

While Grant poured reinforcements into his lines and prepared for an early morning attack on Sunday, Generals Floyd and Pillow unceremoniously dumped total command on General Buckner and fled the fort. When the sole remaining general sent a messenger to Grant proposing terms of evacuation, his old friend responded with a curt demand for unconditional surrender as he insisted he was just about ready to attack. Buckner was shocked at these ungenerous terms, but his army was worn out and almost surrounded so he had little choice but to surrender.

When Ulysses Grant and Simon Bolivar Buckner met on that winter morning, the atmosphere was at first almost as frigid as the weather. Buckner felt betrayed by his Northern friend. However, Grant quickly changed the mood when he offered his old companion his entire purse of money and insisted that

Fort Donelson was situated at a strategic point on the Cumberland River.

the general's wife should be allowed to visit him. Officers were allowed to keep their horses, swords, and pistols and Grant insisted he would attempt to exchange the men for Union prisoners as soon as he could manage it. In turn, Buckner exclaimed that he still loved the "old flag" of the United States that both men had fought under.

However General Buckner returned to the south after being exchanged for a Northern prisoner to fight again for the Confederate flag. His son eventually would fight, and die, for the "old flag" of a united America. General Simon Bolivar Buckner Jr. would become one of the highest-ranking American generals of World War II and command the enormous army that fought the last battle of the war in Okinawa, near mainland Japan. On the other hand, Buckner's old friend and antagonist, Ulysses Grant, was about to embark on a thrilling adventure. When word of Grant's "unconditional surrender" message and the capture of almost 20,000 Confederate soldiers reached the streets of the North, entire towns and cities went wild with the first major Union victory of the war. President Abraham Lincoln quietly penciled this fighting general's name on a list of men who might someday lead the Union to final victory.

III

Vicksburg:
Gibraltar of the West

On the warm, still night of April 16, 1863, 11-year-old Frederick Grant was treated to the kind of fireworks display that most boys his age could only dream about. Fred and his younger brother sat down with their parents on deck chairs onboard the steamer Magnolia as a fantastic display of lights flashed in the sky about three miles away. However, this was no preview of an Independence Day celebration. Fred's father was General Ulysses S. Grant, and at the moment this Yankee commander was desperate to capture the most important piece of real estate in North America, the Mississippi River port city of Vicksburg.

Frederick's father had spent most of the past fall and winter trying to get his army of bluecoats in position to besiege a town that was so well defended that the Confederates called Vicksburg the "Gibraltar of the West" in reference to the impregnable island in Europe. Grant had ordered his men to try digging new waterways around the city, to try frontal attacks

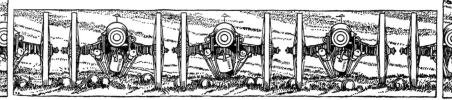

General Ulysses S. Grant commanded the siege of Vicksburg.

against the city's trenches, and to try a dozen more unusual schemes—nothing had worked. The Rebels still sat in Vicksburg and as long as they were there it would be impossible for the North to win the Civil War. Vicksburg was important because by the spring of 1863 the Yankees had control of the entire Mississippi River with the exception of a stretch of about 200 miles between Vicksburg and the town of Port Hudson. As long as the Southerners controlled this stretch of the Mississippi, the Rebel armies in Virginia and Tennessee had access to the large quantities of men, cattle, and cotton that were on the western side of the Mississippi River. However, if Vicksburg was ever captured and the Union controlled the entire Mississippi River, the Confederacy might never recover from the loss.

The light show that Frederick Grant and his parents were watching on this warm spring evening was the brainchild of Commodore David Porter and Ulysses Grant. The two men had hatched a plan in which Porter's fleet of warships would run the Vicksburg batteries at night and, if successful, provide cover for Union transports to ferry the Yankee army from the west bank of the Mississippi River to the east, or Vicksburg, side, several miles below the end of the Confederate trenches. No one was sure whether a Federal warship could survive the plunging fire of the Rebel batteries stationed high on the bluffs, 200 feet above the river, but Porter covered every one of his 11 ships with as much railroad iron and as many cotton bales as he could find.

The fleet steamed southward when it was fully dark, and when the Yankee ships were opposite Vicksburg Rebel lookouts spotted the vessels and gunners rushed to their posts. Moments later a hail of shells were plunging down on the ships, and one, the *Patrick Henry* suddenly caught on fire and blew up only moments after the crew abandoned her. The other 10 ships passed the gauntlet with plenty of assorted holes but still in seaworthy condition, and soon their guns were covering a huge ferrying operation as thousands of bluecoats were landed in the small town of Bruinsburg, Mississippi, well south of Confederate guns. Ulysses S. Grant now put into operation a plan that would receive praise for over a century.

When Grant first crossed over into Mississippi from Louisiana, he actually had fewer troops than his Confederate opponent. The Union commander had about 40,000 men while the Confederate commander of Vicksburg, General John Pemberton, had about 50,000 graycoats under his command. So before Grant could attack Vicksburg directly, he had to cut the odds against him. First, he dispatched Colonel Benjamin Grierson, a former music teacher, with about 1,000 horse soldiers on a gigantic raid that slashed through hundreds of miles of Mississippi countryside. Grierson's men ripped up railroads, cut telegraph

Commodore David Porter led the Union's naval attack on Vicksburg.

lines, and created so much havoc that Pemberton had to send nearly 7,000 men chasing after them. Then, Grant ordered his trusted lieutenant, William Tecumseh Sherman, to launch a mock attack at Vicksburg from north of the city. Sherman enjoyed his chance to become a showman and he deployed dozens of virtually empty "troop trains" and scores of bogus "troop transport ships" in a brilliantly staged "attack" that never quite turned into a real battle. Pemberton rushed thousands of vital troops to stop Sherman's "attack," never realizing that most of Sherman's actual force was being ferried across the Mississippi far to the south. Pemberton had cut his army by a third when he was shocked by messages from scouts that Grant's main army had just showed up in front of the city of Jackson, Mississippi, the capital city and a vital rail center. The bluecoats promptly cut the main rail line between Vicksburg and Jackson and then started marching back toward the Mississippi River from the east. At this point the Confederate general was in a terrible dilemma.

John Pemberton was a rarity for a Confederate general; he was born and raised in Pennsylvania and did not have a trace of a Southern accent. He had married a Southern girl when he was younger, and when the nation began to split in two, the Philadelphia native had decided to cast his lot with the Confederacy. He quickly became very friendly with President Jefferson Davis, and by the spring of 1863 commanded one of the two largest Rebel armies in the field. When his friend President Davis received word of Grant's activities, he told his general to just sit tight in Vicksburg and wait for Confederate relief forces to be sent to his aid. However, Pemberton's immediate superior was Confederate, western-theater commander General Joseph Johnston, a man who loathed Jefferson Davis.

Johnston told Pemberton that it would be impossible to hold Vicksburg once Grant ferried enough men into Mississippi, and the senior general ordered his subordinate to evacuate the city before he found himself trapped.

Pemberton decided on a disastrous compromise. He left half the army in the Vicksburg trenches and marched the other half toward Jackson to confront Grant. In two bloody battles, Champion's Hill and Big Black River, the Rebels were badly beaten by the larger Yankee army and by the middle of May, the mangled survivors were pouring back into Vicksburg with the victorious Federals right behind them. Now it was Grant's turn to make a major mistake. The Union general was convinced that the retreating Confederates had no fight left in them after two major defeats and decided that if he smashed into Vicksburg's defenses before the Rebels could catch their breath he could raise the Stars and Stripes over the town almost immediately. However, half of the Confederate soldiers had remained in the town during these battles and were both well-rested and convinced they could hold the city. A series of forts had been built in an arc from Fort Hill north of the town to South Fort on the Mississippi River three miles south of the city. Each of the six main roads into Vicksburg was guarded by a powerful fort and the forts were connected to one another by a continuous line of ramparts and rifle pits. Beyond these formidable inner defenses was a continuous ditch 8 feet deep and 14 feet wide which in turn was fronted by rows of sharpened stakes and rows of strung out telegraph wire.

General Grant arrived in front of these impressive defenses on the evening of May 18 and ordered the regiments that had marched in with him to attack the next afternoon. However, right from the start, it

William Tecumseh Sherman fought alongside General Grant at the siege of Vicksburg.

became obvious that the graycoats weren't as vulnerable as Grant thought. Rebel defenders poured musket fire into the Yankee attackers and rolled primitive hand grenades down on the bluecoats as they tried to push through the trenches. General Sherman insisted that "the Rebel parapets were strongly manned and the enemy fought hard and well." In not much more than an hour over 1,000 Federals were dead or wounded compared to fewer than 100 Rebels and Grant ordered a withdrawal. Three days later the Yankees were smashing against Vicskburg's fortifications once again and the results were no better. On this stifling Friday morning thousands of bluecoats climbed over sharpened stakes, pushed through muddy ditches, and clambered up the steep walls of Rebel parapets. Many of these men never returned to their own camps.

In one of the most heavily fortified parts of the Confederate lines a force of Texans had been equipped with six loaded muskets apiece to hit the Yankees with an almost non-stop fire when they approached the parapets. As one of Sherman's regiments sprinted forward, entire ranks of bluecoats went down in the sheet of flame. One Texan remarked that "as fast as hands could gather them up, one after another, the muskets were brought to bear. The blue lines vanished amid fearful slaughter." As the Union attack force almost disintegrated, one solitary bluecoat picked up the fallen regimental flag and kept charging the Texan position completely alone. The defenders were so moved by this incredibly fearless act that men yelled to one another, "Don't shoot at that brave man again, he is too brave to be killed that way!" As the single Yankee reached the parapet, Confederate soldiers grabbed him by the arms and pulled him down to safety. A moment later Rebels were surrounding this blue-coated celebrity, shaking his hand and congratulating him on his miraculous escape. Unfortunately, over 3,000 other Federal soldiers were not so lucky and their bodies covered the approaches to Vicksburg while the Rebels had lost only 500 men.

Ulysses Grant was hardly enthusiastic about conducting a traditional siege, but he realized that he could still get plenty of reinforcements and rations while his opponent could receive few of either of these things. Union soldiers, Confederate defenders, and Vicksburg civilians now settled down to a grim siege that dragged through the next six weeks. While the bluecoats had plenty of food and enough troops to rotate duty in and out of the siege lines, Pemberton's men had little rest and even less food. The only meat available was tough mule steak and rancid bacon while most men had to settle for a mush concoction of ground peas and cornmeal. One soldier complained with disgust, "it made a nauseous composition as the corn-meal cooked in half the time as the peas-meal so the stuff was half raw and had the properties of India Rubber." Some fortunate Confederate soldiers were able to trade Southern tobacco for Yankee coffee, but most graycoats had to make do with a strange beverage that was a mixture of ground sweet potatoes, blackberry beans, and sassafras roots.

Within a week or two, Vicksburg's civilians were eating even less tasty meals than the soldiers. Thousands of Southerners had poured into the town to escape Grant's advancing Yankees, and food stocks were almost exhausted. Union artillery and gunboats pounded the city, and as citizens huddled in basements or caves dug out of the many cliffs, food became the main topic of conversation. Butchers started advertising that cats, dogs, and even rats were almost as good as chicken and many customers didn't have the courage to identify too closely the origin of the meat they had just purchased.

By early July of 1863 Pemberton's army was on the brink of starvation, and the general started thinking about the terms he could get from Grant if he surrendered the city. Finally, on July 3, almost at the exact time that George Pickett's graycoats were being slaughtered on Cemetery Ridge in far off Gettysburg, Pemberton and Grant sat on a log under a tree between the two siege lines and discussed terms. Pemberton was convinced that Grant was so anxious to finalize a surrender by Independence Day that he held out for very generous conditions. The Yankee

general didn't disappoint him. Grant insisted that if the Rebels would surrender immediately, the entire Confederate army would be paroled on the spot and permitted to go home; all officers could keep their swords, pistols, and horses. The Confederate commander quickly accepted these terms, and the next morning, on July 4, 1863, Ulysses S. Grant was able to inform a grateful Abraham Lincoln that the American

Union soldiers spent weeks in the trenches before Vicksburg.

39

flag now flew over Vicksburg's city hall. The president watched citizens celebrate in the streets of Washington and wrote concerning the victory and the Mississippi River that with the fall of Vicksburg "the Father of Waters again goes unvexed to the sea."

IV

Fort Wagner:
Bloodstains in the Sand

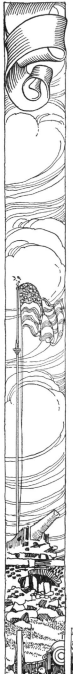

*T*he surrender of Vicksburg on July 4, 1863, was greeted with wild celebrations all over the Northern states. One of the most important spots in the Confederacy now flew the Stars and Stripes again. Now Northerners hoped that cities such as Atlanta and Richmond would be captured in the near future. However, no city in the South had the level of emotional impact on both Southerners and Northerners alike as the beautiful port of Charleston, South Carolina. Southerners viewed the town as the birthplace of the Confederacy while Northerners were convinced that it was the most wicked place in America. One Yankee admiral insisted, "As Boston was regarded as the cradle of American liberty, so Charleston was considered the nursery of disunion. During our Civil War no city in the South was so obnoxious to Union men as Charleston."

After the spectacular Union victories at Vicksburg and Gettysburg, most Northerners shifted their attention to South Carolina where a Yankee fleet and army

Union sharpshooters waited for battle in the sands by Fort Wagner.

General Quincy A. Gillmore was one of the generals ordered to capture the city of Charleston.

were preparing to attempt the capture of Charleston. Two years earlier, at the opening of the Civil War, Fort Sumter had been seen as the key to control of the harbor and the city and now in the summer of 1863, it was the Yankees who were planning to bombard and capture the legendary fort. However, the Rebels had enjoyed a long period of time to prepare for the Federal attack and they had made one major improvement since 1861 which was to build another fortification that covered one of the main approaches to Fort Sumter—Fort Wagner. The two men charged by President Lincoln to capture Charleston, Admiral Samuel DuPont and General Quincy Gillmore knew that Charleston could never be forced to surrender until Fort Sumter was once again under Union control, and Sumter could never be captured unless Fort Wagner was taken. Therefore, for much of the summer of 1863 this fort of sand and dirt walls on the tip of Morris Island would be one of the most fought over pieces of land in America.

On July 9, 1863, five days after the surrender of Vicksburg, the Yankee campaign against Fort Wagner got underway. In the hot, sultry twilight of this Thursday evening a storming party of blue-coats under General George Strong was rowed from Union held Folly Island to the south shore of Morris Island. By Friday morning the Yankees had captured most of the island as they pushed inland under the cover of 47 land artillery pieces and four monitor-class warships. The person who was the most concerned about this Yankee advance was the Confederate commander of Charleston, General Pierre Beauregard. The Louisianan, who had captured Fort Sumter from the Federals two years earlier, was now responsible for defending the fort and he knew that control of Fort Wagner might be the key to the upcoming battle. The colorful general quickly poured more Rebel troops into Fort Wagner until more than 1,000 men and 20 cannons were spread out along the sandy parapets. Beauregard knew that the Yankees now had more men on Morris Island than the graycoat defenders but he also knew that the men in Fort Wagner had a huge advantage. The fort had been built on the most narrow part of the island, and the front walls of the structure stretched almost the whole distance from the ocean on one side of the island to the swampy marshes on the other side. Union attackers could only charge directly at the front of Fort Wagner and the Rebels could place every rifleman and cannon to cover that single wall. The Yankees would quickly

General George C. Strong landed Union forces on Morris Island ready to assault Fort Wagner.

The Union navy bombarded Fort Wagner from the sea while the army bombarded from land.

find out how important that Confederate advantage really was. On Saturday, July 11, General Gillmore ordered an Union assault on Fort Wagner and the charging bluecoats were met by a sheet of musket fire and artillery fire that ripped through the men like a metallic sleet storm. Whole units seemed to be almost blown away by the furious Rebel firepower and Gillmore called the fiasco off.

Now, as dead and wounded bluecoats were carried from the beach, the first stage of the siege of Fort Wagner got underway. Yankee engineers and gunners put 41 huge siege guns and siege mortars into place a mile from the fort and began pounding the walls day and night. At the same time, the Union navy sailed up and down past the ocean side of Fort Wagner pouring the massed fire of its ships at the parapets. However,

Confederate engineers had filled the fort with a network of bombproof shelters which allowed the defenders to sit under cover and let the Yankees try to do their worst.

For more than a week citizens in Charleston, Rebel soldiers guarding Fort Sumter, and Union infantrymen on Morris Island watched the fantastic display of firepower while everyone wondered how badly damaged Fort Wagner really was. Finally, General Gillmore decided that it was time for a ground assault and a powerful attack force of 10 regiments containing over 6,000 men was given orders to seize the fort. The Union commander felt that the best chance for a successful assault was at night, when, hopefully, Confederate gunners and riflemen would have a hard time spotting the advancing bluecoats.

In the late afternoon of July 18, 1863, the assault regiments were lined up in attack formation about a mile across the beach from the parapets of Fort Wagner. The island was so narrow that only one regiment at a time could advance toward the fort and even with the cover of darkness there was a good chance that the first unit in line would be slaughtered. Despite this awful danger, Colonel Robert Gould Shaw volunteered his unit, the 54th Massachusetts Infantry, to be the lead regiment in the daring assault. Shaw and his men were already becoming famous since the regiment was one of the first units of African Americans

General Pierre Beauregard was the Confederate commander of Charleston and was responsible for the defense of Forts Sumter and Wagner.

enrolled in the Union army and only a few days earlier several companies of these black volunteers had successfully fought off a vicious Rebel attempt to retake Morris Island. Now these men faced an even bloodier battle.

The commander of one of the three assault brigades, Colonel Haldimind Putnam, was convinced that the operation was suicidal and insisted to his superiors that "we are all going into Wagner like a flock of sheep." However, as the sun set on this summer afternoon, the 54th Massachusetts and its backup regiments started marching at quick time toward the looming parapets. One of the Massachusetts regimental officers was Lieutenant Garth James, the brother of famous writers Henry and William James. The young lieutenant was shocked at how little cover there would be along the stretch of sandy beach that lay between his men and the walls of Fort Wagner, but he insisted, "the men had no doubt they should follow Colonel Shaw wherever they were led."

At around 8 P.M. on this Saturday evening the bluecoat attackers sprinted toward Wagner's parapets. Sergeant Lewis Douglass, son of the noted African American writer and abolitionist, Frederick Douglass, noted proudly, "not a man flinched although it was a trying time. Men fell all around me. A shell would explode and clear a space of twenty feet; our men would close up again." Three regiments of North Carolina troops lined up every musket and cannon they could deploy along Fort Wagner's front wall and produced what Sergeant Douglass called "a perfect hail of shot and shell" while a Union officer insisted "sheets of flame darted from every corner and embrasure."

As Colonel Shaw and several of his men attempted to scramble up the sandy wall, the young commander was shot in the chest and then dropped riddled with several more bullets. As Shaw was dying, Colonel Putnam led his men into knee-deep water to try to get around to the fort's side wall but this colonel was soon dead as well and as the bluecoats splashed through the rolling waves, reserve units in Fort Wagner began picking them off by the score. A few minutes later the commander of the assault force, General Strong, was cut down trying to rally his men and soon everyone on both sides sensed the attack had failed.

The Federals had paid a fearsome price for this gallant but futile attack. A casualty list of 246 killed, 890 wounded, and 391 captured far exceeded the 167 men lost among the defenders. The 54th Massachusetts alone had lost 256 men including its colonel and every company commander, and two other regiments from New York and Connecticut had lost almost as many troops. General Gillmore decided to suspend any further attacks until he could position his cannons and mortars at almost point-blank range and literally blast the walls of Fort Wagner to pieces. For the next six weeks Federal engineers built siege lines closer and closer to the fort while the Union navy pounded Fort Sumter's guns to prevent that fort from interfering with a new assault on its covering post. By the evening of September 6, every single cannon in Fort Sumter had been knocked out of action and Union engineers were digging trenches almost in front of Fort Wagner's front moat. An order for a new assault was issued for the next morning, but during the night the Confederates evacuated every soldier and every cannon that could be moved. When the bluecoats rushed the parapets at dawn on September 7, they were met by silence. Fort Wagner had been captured, Fort Sumter had been blown into a pile of rubble. Yet, the troops and ships that would be used to finish the

The interior of Fort Sumter during the bombardment from Morris Island was in sharp contrast to its interior prior to the war (page 17).

job and capture Charleston were suddenly needed elsewhere and ordered to leave and the Confederate flag would wave over the birthplace of secessionism almost until the end of the war. The capture of Fort Wagner was a Union victory, but one of the most hollow victories of the war.

V

Fort Fisher:
Last Gateway to the Confederacy

One of the few high-ranking Union officers who was involved in the attack on Fort Wagner and was still more or less in one piece at the end would later become one of the central figures in an even more spectacular battle for a fort. Galusha Pennypacker was only 18 years old when the Yankees attempted to storm Fort Wagner and most people thought that he looked more like 15. However, Pennypacker was the youngest regimental commander in the Union army and had already become a legendary figure. His grandfather had been a high-ranking officer in the American army during the War of Independence and his family home in Pennsylvania had been used as George Washington's headquarters for an entire winter. His family members were prominent abolitionists before the Civil War and his house was a station on the "Underground Railroad" for escaping slaves. Pennypacker had volunteered for the Union army at 16 and by the end of 1863 had been wounded 13 times and was commander of the 97th Pennsylvania

Fort Fisher was built to withstand heavy bombardment, with walls 9 feet high and 25 feet thick.

Regiment which was considered one of the best units in the Federal army. Within another year the teenager would become involved in a campaign that would nearly end his life and yet make him a general before he was even old enough to vote.

As the year 1864 came to a close, the Confederacy was moving very rapidly towards defeat. During the last few months, General William Sherman had captured the vital city of Atlanta and was now marching through Georgia devastating that state; the main Confederate army in the west, under General John Hood had been almost annihilated in the battles of Franklin and Nashville; and the mighty Army of Northern Virginia was now besieged in a long trench line that stretched from Petersburg to the Confederate capital of Richmond. Since much of the Confederacy was now occupied by Federal troops, Southern supply officers were forced to depend more and more on provisions and equipment that could be shipped in from Europe onboard the daring blockade runners that could slip through the ring of Yankee ships that guarded the Rebel coastline. However, by December of 1864 almost every important Southern harbor had been captured by the Federals so that only the port city of Wilmington, North Carolina, remained open for business in the blockade-running trade.

Wilmington was now the last window to the outside world for a dying Confederacy and if the Union ever captured the city, Lee's besieged army would be forced to evacuate Richmond. In order to prevent this disaster from happening, Confederate engineers had

General Benjamin Butler developed a bold plan to blow up Fort Fisher.

built one of the strongest forts in the world at the point where the Cape Fear River flowed into the Atlantic Ocean. This structure was named Fort Fisher and it had been built with walls 9 feet high and 25 feet thick, designed to absorb the fire of almost any cannon of the time. The fort's commander, Colonel William Lamb, had access to 47 cannons and mortars including one powerful battery mounted on a 60-foot-high sand mound that could plunge huge shells on ships far below. Fort Fisher was constructed with a main seaside wall that faced the Atlantic Ocean and stretched for nearly a mile while the main, land-side wall was built to deter attack from the miles of scrubby beach that extended north of the fort.

On paper, Fort Fisher seemed to be impregnable, but by the last few weeks of 1864, General Ulysses S. Grant started to believe that it was just possible that this key Rebel fortress and the city it protected were ripe for capture. General Grant was now the commanding general of all United States armies and had spent most of the past year jousting with General Robert E. Lee in the woods and fields of Virginia. The Union general had finally pinned his opponent to a huge series of trench lines around the Confederate capital, but Grant was bored by siege warfare and was looking around for some daring operation that might break the stalemate at Richmond. At this point, General Benjamin Butler offered his commander an exciting plan. Butler was a political leader from Massachusetts who had received an appointment as a Union general and had been responsible for more Yankee defeats than victories. Now the cross-eyed, raspy-voiced general approached Grant with a plan to capture Fort Fisher by beaching a Union ship filled with explosives near the fort's walls and once the defenses were blown up in the blast, pouring bluecoat troops into the helpless stronghold. Grant was intrigued about the possibilities of this daring plan, and on December 13, 1864, the largest fleet that had ever been assembled under the American flag set sail from Hampton Roads, Virginia, and headed for North Carolina.

The expedition to capture Fort Fisher included over 7,000 assault troops carried on dozens of transport vessels while 57 warships including frigates, monitors, and gunboats carrying hundreds of cannons hovered protectively nearby. The key ship in the expedition was the USS *Louisiana*, a Federal warship that had been rebuilt to resemble a Confederate blockade runner and crammed with over 200 tons of gunpowder to demolish the Rebel fort's walls. The commanders of the expedition were General Butler and Admiral David Dixon Porter, the feisty sailor who had run the Confederate gauntlet at Vicksburg.

After several delays caused by winter storms, the Union fleet appeared before Fort Fisher on the day before Christmas Eve and Colonel Lamb shuddered at the huge armada facing him. A Confederate government that was desperate to stop Sherman's March to the Sea had stripped Fort Fisher

Admiral David Dixon Porter led the naval assault against Fort Fisher.

of most of its garrison until only 500 regular soldiers still remained on the fort's walls. Just before the Yankee fleet arrived, the governor of North Carolina had rushed 450 "junior reserves," 16- and 17-year-old boys, to the fort along with a few companies of militiamen. However, Lamb's best hope was coming from Richmond. General Robert E. Lee was so concerned that the capture of Wilmington and Fort Fisher would cut his shaky supply line that he had ordered General Robert Hoke's entire division of 6,000 Confederate troops to board trains and head south for Wilmington. However, the southern rail system was now so worn out that the graycoat soldiers were enduring a long series of detours on their way to North Carolina and Colonel Lamb would be on his own to face the upcoming Yankee attack.

At a few minutes past midnight on a clear, cold Christmas Eve, the Federal operation against Fort

Fisher lurched into action. Commander Alexander Rhind and a small crew of volunteer sailors sailed the powder boat *Louisiana* toward the looming Carolina seashore. The naval officer ordered the anchor dropped when the ship was 250 yards from the beach and carefully set three clockwork timers to ignite the explosives in exactly 90 minutes. Then, just in case all three timers malfunctioned, the young Yankee mariner set fire to the ship's wheelhouse and ordered his crew to abandon ship and row toward a rescue steamer nearby. Admiral Porter was so sure that the blast would be monumental that he had ordered the whole fleet to pull 12 miles off shore to avoid destruction.

Hundreds of blue-coated sailors and soldiers lined the decks of the mighty fleet as they watched and waited for the explosion which was set to go off just past 1:30 A.M. However, all three timers did malfunctioned and it took awhile longer for Rhind's backup plan to work. Finally, at about 2:00, the wheelhouse fire reached the gunpowder and an enormous explosion rocked the still night air. Sailors saw a huge cloud of thick, black smoke heading directly for the fleet while a powerful odor of sulphur reminded many men of descriptions of the atmosphere of hell. Unfortunately for the Yankee plan, the main force of the blast was directed out to sea, not inland, and Fort Fisher was barely scratched by the spectacular explosion. In fact, Rebel troops were convinced that the blast was actually caused by a Federal warship being ripped apart by an exploding boiler.

Christmas Eve and Christmas Day were noisy events around Fort Fisher as Admiral Porter fired over 10,000 shells at the walls and Benjamin Butler landed 2,000 of his men to test the fort's land defenses. However, when it became obvious that the bombard-

General Alfred H. Terry was chosen to take over command of the Union assault of Fort Fisher.

ment had caused almost no damage and Confederate prisoners insisted that General Hoke was preparing to attack Butler's landing force from behind, the whole operation was called off and the fleet steamed north to Virginia. When Porter brusquely told his old friend Grant of Butler's incompetence in the operation, the Union commander promptly sacked the Massachusetts politician, appointed General Alfred Terry in his place, and reinforced the expedition with two new brigades of black soldiers. Soon after New Year's Day of 1865, the fleet was headed south again with orders to not return until Fort Fisher was flying the Stars and Stripes. Soon the tide was turning much more in favor of the Yankees.

Casemates were built into the walls of forts for the safe firing of cannons.

On January 13, 1865, the Federal assault force was back in front of Fort Fisher, and this time each commander appeared to know exactly what he had to do to capture the Rebel stronghold. Admiral Porter changed the whole mission of his bombardment squadrons and ordered his gunners to ignore the walls in favor of knocking out the fort's cannons and riflemen. For two days the Union warships pounded Colonel Lamb's main batteries of infantry units and soon a large number of men and well over half the guns were out of action.

Sunday, January 15, dawned crystal clear and bright, although the temperature was a very chilly 33 degrees as the blue-coated troops prepared to attack. General Terry had not repeated General Butler's mistake of only throwing in part of his army; the new commander had spent the past two days supervising the unloading of well over 8,000 men for a powerful full-scale assault. One of the three main attack brigades was under the command of Galusha Pennypacker who had gone from the army's youngest regimental commander to the army's youngest brigade commander. Almost 3,000 men were being led by a person who was just leaving his teenage years behind. Admiral Porter had offered to strengthen the assault by ordering over 2,000 sailors and marines to storm the sea side of the fort in order to distract the defenders from Terry's land-side operation.

When Colonel Lamb saw the Federal soldiers and sailors massing to attack his fort, his best hope for aid lay with the 6,000 Confederates of General Hoke's division who were now under the overall command of General Braxton Bragg. Bragg, who was as controversial in the South as Ben Butler was in the North, had deployed this powerful force along a ridge called Sugarloaf Hill about two miles north of the main Union attack force. Colonel Lamb was convinced that if his garrison could just hold on for awhile, Bragg could order this large force to annihilate the Yankees from the rear.

Admiral Porter ordered one final bombardment of the fleet, and then, at just past 2 P.M. on this short winter day, the attack force of sailors and marines landed on the beach and prepared to "board" Fort Fisher as if they were boarding an enemy ship. The gray-coated defenders were ready for this attack and within a few minutes over 300 men were sprawled among the sand dunes, victims of a wall of musket and artillery fire. However, their sacrifice was not in vain as the attack distracted the Rebels long enough for the Union infantry force to close in on the fort from the land side.

Galusha Pennypacker was a hero of the battle of Fort Fisher and became the youngest general in the U.S. army.

The two leading Union brigades, led by Colonel Newton Curtis and Galusha Pennypacker sprinted over the last few hundred yards of sandy ground and began scrambling up the steep walls of Fort Fisher. Hundreds of screaming Yankees, led by their brigade commanders, poured over the fort's walls and began one of the most furious hand to hand fights of the war. Men were so close together that they didn't have room to load their rifles and used rifle butts and fists instead. Colonel Curtis went down when a Confederate cannon shell exploded just above him, ripping out one eye and horribly mangling his face. Pennypacker, waving the flag of his old regiment, was the first man over one of the fort's walls but was shot through the hip and carried off with what appeared to be a mortal wound.

The Confederates fought desperately for every square foot of their fort and the Federals paid in blood for every strong point they captured. However, although Colonel Lamb pleaded for General Bragg to launch a rear attack on the Yankees, the grizzled general grimly held his ground while the garrison was overwhelmed by thousands of bluecoats. Soon Lamb joined Curtis and Pennypacker on the seriously wounded list and gradually as darkness covered the fort, the Rebel defenders surrendered.

The next morning as the Stars and Stripes were raised over the battered walls of Fort Fisher, a final tragedy occurred. Two Union troops looking for souvenirs carried candles into a room they didn't know was the main powder magazine of the fort. A spectacular explosion lifted dozens of men right off the ground and buried scores of others below tons of sand, adding another 200 fatalities to an already bloody battle. At a cost of 1,400 men killed and

wounded, General Terry and Admiral Porter had closed off the last gateway to the outside world open to the Confederacy and captured nearly 2,000 Rebels in the process. Galusha Pennypacker was taken back to a Federal field hospital where he was initially told he was dying. However, he staged a miraculous recovery and became one of the most prominent heroes of the battle of Fort Fisher. Not only did he receive the Congressional Medal of Honor, he was also promoted to become the youngest general in the United States army.

One of the guns of Fort Fisher, broken during the bombardment.

The struggle for these strongholds during the Civil War eventually had a major role in the outcome of the contest between North and South. These were some of the bloodiest engagements of the conflict between Union and Confederacy and yet once the war ended men in both blue and gray could share the pride in their roles in the battles fought for these places. Forty years after the war ended men such as William Lamb, the commander of Fort Fisher, Newton Curtis and Galusha Pennypacker, the Yankee assault commanders, and James Parker, an officer leading the navy and marine attackers, could all agree on how dramatic their confrontations had been to both Federals and Confederates. On a bright winter day four decades after the guns had been silenced, Colonel Lamb placed his arms around his old adversaries and exclaimed, "Thank God we stand here today as friends!"

Glossary

battery	A grouping of artillery pieces; an artillery unit within an army.
blockade	A military maneuver in which supply and information sources are cut off to a city or harbor.
blockade runner	A ship or person that tries to break through a blockade to bring supplies and information.
bluecoats	Term used for soldiers in the Northern Union army during the Civil War because of the color of their uniform.
casemate	A fortified area within a fort from which guns are fired through a small opening.
Confederacy	The Southern states that seceded from the Union formed a new country called the Confederate States of America also called the Confederacy.
Federals	A name used for members of the Union.
graycoats	Term used for soldiers in the Southern Confederate army during the Civil War because of the color of their uniform.
parapet	A wall or elevation of dirt or stone built to protect soldiers during enemy attack.
rampart	A wall-like ridge or embankment built as a fortification against enemy troops.
Rebels	Term used for Southerners in the Civil War.
secessionist	Southerners who voted to secede from the Union and form their own republic.
siege	A military strategy usually against a city in which it is surrounded by enemy troops and ships and all supply routes are cut off. Usually used to try to get a city to surrender.
Stars and Stripes	The flag of the United States.
Union	The United States of America.
Yankees	Term used for Northerners during the Civil War.

Further Reading

Beauregard, Pierre. "The Defense of Charleston." *Battles and Leaders of the Civil War*, Vol. IV. Thomas Yoseloff, 1956.

Cooling, Banjamin. *Forts Henry and Donelson: The Key to the Confederate Heartland*. University of Tennessee Press, 1987.

Doubleday, Abner. *Reminiscences of Forts Sumter and Moultrie in 1860-61*. Harper Brothers, 1876.

Gragg, Rod. *Confederate Goliath: The Battle of Fort Fisher*. Harper Collins, 1991.

Grant, Ulysses. S. *Personal Memoirs*. Harper Brothers, 1885.

Websites About Civil War Forts

Fort Fisher: statelibrary.dcr.state.nc.us/ncsites/fisher.htm

Fort Sumter: www.nps.gov/fosu

Fort Donelson: www.nps.gov/fodo

Fort Pillow: americancivilwar.com/statepic/tn/tn030.html

Fort Moultrie: www.nps.gov/fomo

Crisis at Fort Sumter: www.tulane.edu/~latner

54th Massachusetts: www.nara.gov/exhall/originals/54thmass.html

Vicksburg: americancivilwar.com/statepic/ms/ms011.html
    members.xoom.com/civilwar/vicks.htm
    www.americancivilwar.com/vicks.html

Index

PHOTO CREDITS

Harper's Weekly : pp. 10, 14, 17, 18, 22, 24, 25, 26, 29, 39, 42, 43, 44, 48, 55, 56; Library of Congress:
    pp. 12, 15, 16, 32, 33, 36, 50, 58, 59; National Archives: pp. 27, 45, 51, 53